You Can Make Money as an Author

Jump on the Bandwagon & Cash In Now!

By

Bob Carpenter

This book contains business strategies, marketing methods and other business ideas that, without regard to my own results and experience, may not produce the same, similar or any results for you. Bob Carpenter makes no guarantee, either expressed or implied, that following the advice or content of this book, or from his website or provided by Bob Carpenter by any other method, will cause you to make money or improve your profits because there are many factors beyond your, or my control that affect any given business, business procedure or strategy. Your results will depend upon the nature of your product, service and business practices, as well as the conditions of the marketplace, your experience, outlook, methods, and situations that are beyond your or my control.

As with any business venture you assume all risk related to your use of your money, at your own risk.

Dedication

With all due respect and sincerity, I would like to dedicate this book to you, my reader. It is your support that is making this work successful. I hope that, in return, I have delivered information above and beyond your expectations. You are the only judge of that. Thank you very much.

Acknowledgements

I would like to publicly thank my late parents for their part in sharing stories and facts and figures from their youth with me that have provided valuable insights for this book

Additionally, I would like to offer my heartfelt thanks to Warren Buffett, Kim Komando, the late Steve Jobs, Steve Harrison, John S. Rhodes and Jay Boyer. I thank you all for going before me and speaking about your journey, thereby enabling me to "stand on your shoulders" and see further and more clearly than I could have without your help. Thank you very much.

Finally, but far from least, I would like to thank my friend, The late First Sergeant Dan Moore for guiding me to reading when I was young, as well as my wonderful wife, Glocil Carpenter for her patience with me during the writing process and for her loving kindness and thoughtful suggestions.

All of you have, without realizing it, helped to make this book what it is, and to help me get it published. Thank you!

Table of Contents

Introduction

There is a revolution going on right now. It is a global revolution and was created by technology. This technology has changed and is continuing to change the way things are done. It is in the process of obliterating manufacturing and business as we have known it through the twentieth century. This is simply a fact that cannot be ignored. It is like a wild horse, in a herd of wild horses that have been rounded up by the old time cowboys; this horse demonstrates spirit that is far above the others, and the wise old cowboy knows that he will have an outstanding horse, if he can harness and ride this *one* from a herd of many. This book is about how you can harness this wild horse, technology, and vastly improve your lot in life.

While there are parts of the "Old school" that are crumbling, there are parts of it that will, hopefully, endure and withstand this technological storm.

The old school values of honesty and integrity, kindness, gentleness, and love are still valued and profitable for all; however technology has even changed the ways in which these virtuous qualities are exercised.

If you have ever looked back with 20/20 hindsight and wished that you had seen the opportunities that others embraced, before it was well defined, or even scoffed at, you will find this book is like having a guide in the wilderness who can point things out that your untrained eye doesn't see. I will present you the opportunity to see things that most people are missing, affording you the opportunity to ride an exciting and lucrative wave of the future, with little or no risk.

Chapter 1

The Old School

The "Old School" is where I come from. It was a good school and served me well. The values of honesty, integrity, love, gentleness and kindness to others that it taught me are enduring values that are still valued today. I am thankful for that. On the other hand, the business lessons, the occupational lessons, that I learned in the old school are, for the most part, in the throes of death, because of technology. As is natural in the course of human events, the old ways are perishing and the future looks very different from the past.

If we are to prosper in the times ahead, we will have to make the adjustment, whether we like it or not. That's just a fact. Looking back through my parent's life, I was able to learn that lesson.

My mother and father were born in 1918 and 1917, respectively. They were born during the early stages of the industrial revolution, a time during which the United States was making great strides of growth and industrial and economic development. World War I had just ended; America had endured a great crisis. My parents also lived through the great depression, my father fought in World War II, they made it through the recession and stagflation of the 1970's. That's interesting, but what did they see in their lifetimes?

When they were born, a look out the window at the streets revealed people bustling about mostly on foot, many traveling by horse and wagon, or on horseback, and just a privileged few riding in early automobiles, such as the Model T Ford. There were virtually no airplanes in the sky; no airports. Ships and railroads were the prime movers of goods.

The opportunities afforded by the industrial revolution moved quickly. Before they were thirty years old, they, themselves, traveled by car, and even owned one. Before long they flew in a commercial airplane (my first flight at about age 6), they went on to see Neil Armstrong become the man on the moon. They experienced the introduction of the marvels of the telephone, television, the advent of the hand held calculator, the marvels of the desktop computer and cell phones. They saw trucks take freight from the railroads and planes take passengers from the ships. As they continued through their journey on this planet, they saw more than they could have ever imagined. They eschewed the changes, even as they embraced many of them, but even though they embraced some of those changes, they never imagined that they could seize the opportunity that accompanied those changes.

> "Other than God and the laws of physics, the only thing that doesn't change is that everything changes." – Bob Carpenter

In their time, the old school of business was in session. It was vibrant and was only open to people who had money, power, or both. Seizing the opportunities of the future would have been more difficult and more risky for them than it is for us today.

The old school was good, and it lives in my memory with the fondness of times gone by.

Today there is a "New school." It is a vibrant, exciting school, teeming with young life that is teaching the new generation the ways of the future. It is overcoming the shortcomings that were difficulties in the old school. The new school is brimming with opportunity, unlike anything that has ever been seen before. Through the products that the new school has produced, the social and monetary barriers that isolated so many in the old school have been broken down, just as God has broken down the "Middle wall of partition" between the Jews and the Gentiles. Just as God has made all to be "partakers of one body," the new school has produced technology that enables anyone who will embrace it to partake of its bounty. The social and financial barriers of the old school are gone. Technology has made it possible to put them into the past.

The new school has made hard, physical work almost obsolete, by providing a viable means for smart work to prevail. Under the doctrine of the old school, hard work was necessary and a way of life for the everyday person. Under the doctrine of the new school, the everyday person can harness the power of technology and earn a living by working smart, and relegating hard work to hired help, or to the status of a hobby.

I love hard work and engage in it almost daily. It is good to keep a body fit and moving, but I am very happy to be able to earn money by working smart. I do hard work mostly for fun. It helps me to age more gracefully.

In the past, most people earned their livings through hard physical work; in the future earnings will be made through smart work, with technology being the medium of accomplishment. As of this writing, April, 2015, I can see that the business and industrial world is a sort of hybrid; a combination of the old and the new. The old is dying and the new is growing stronger and stronger. That process will, at some point, shift business and industry wholly, or almost so, into the ways of the future, the new way, the technological way, the smart way.

Chapter 2

Amazing Technology

A quick review of technology and the attitudes that accompanied its introduction will reveal an abundance of valuable information for us, as we attempt to bring opportunities that are on the horizon into focus.

Back in the 1980's, few, if any, of the "experts" believed that there would ever be a market for the desktop computer, then the desktop computer became commonplace. Hewlett Packard developed the desk top printer, and the "experts" again said that no one would want a printer on their desktop; soon there were desktop printers on virtually every desk in every office. Cell phones were introduced in large bags and a few business people had one in their cars, but the experts said they weren't really a good idea because there are pay phones everywhere. Now there are virtually no pay phones outside of museums and cell phones are in just about everyone's pocket or purse. Note that those who resist change, especially inevitable change usually get left behind.

When I was about 11 years old, I was walking with a buddy of mine. We were embarked on a journey of about a mile and a half to the drug store to cash in some soda bottles, buy some candy and play Johnny Horton's *Battle of New Orleans* on the jukebox at the store. As we walked, I said to my buddy "I figure some day we will be able to have a T.V. set that we can carry in our pockets." At that time the only T.V.'s we knew about were huge. I still don't know what made me think that, but in spite of his objections, saying how impossible that would be, today I have a T.V. that I can carry in my pocket. It's called a Smart Phone.

What we see in our rear view mirror is that the desktop computers were predicted to bomb, along with desktop printers, cell phones and many other things. We can also see that desktop computers turned into laptops, laptops morphed into tablets, and, for the moment, tablets and smart phones are sharing the stage, but now the iWatch is entering at stage right.

Apparently, the naysayers and so-called experts that predicted the failures of all those technological products were fixed on the way things were at the times they were introduced and were unable to see the way things could be, and might become. The people who brought these new and now indispensable products to market, simply used their imaginations to create the future they wanted and probably changed the future for all of us in the process. Don't inhibit your imagination!

Where do we go from here? Good question; read on.

Chapter 3

Opportunities Available Now

With the advent of the latest technological marvels of our time, come wonderful opportunities that are available to anyone who seizes them. And I mean literally anyone.

Let's not start by making excuses. If you don't own and can't afford to buy a computer, you can use one at most libraries, you can team up with someone who does own one. If you are blind, you can team up with a sighted friend or family member. Literally anyone with a little determination can seize these opportunities by harnessing today's technology. If you are disadvantaged you may need to apply a little more determination, but you can do it. The question for all is will you do it?

Along with the new technology, companies have sprouted up that harness its power and they are changing the way business is conducted. These companies will play a key role in your effort to harness the technology and cash in on the boom.

One such company is Amazon. From start to finish, they do business the modern way. Amazon has been so successful that their success pushed the discount store giant, Wal-Mart, to create a virtual online shopping experience for their customers. How does this apply to you? I'm glad you asked.

Amazon wants to partner with you to bring your product to market! You don't have to beg, grovel or worry about being rejected if you want to bring a decent product that has value for your target audience to market. Amazon will do almost everything for you. Almost everything! Amazon is "New school." They do business the modern way; the way of the future. It has created a wave of prosperity that you can ride all the way to the bank!

This book is an example of my partnership with Amazon. I wrote the book, I own the material. Amazon produces the book, markets the book, sells the book, collects the money, delivers the goods for me and keeps only a small percentage of the gross sales. The only thing Amazon didn't do for me was read my mind, write & format the book.

Everyone has a story to tell; everyone has a book between their ears. What I have done with this book, you can do with your story or book. All you have to do to start is to search the internet for a term like "publishing a book with amazon." Click and read how they do it. Read about how little you have to do. This is modern technology at work in a very meaningful way, to put it mildly.

If you are an entertainer, you can publish CD's and DVD's on Amazon.

Why in the world would Amazon do this? I cannot give you a definitive answer, but I am sure that they do it because it helps them have a much larger line of products and books to offer, which leads to more shoppers, more sales and more income.

Guess what? Amazon has harnessed the modern technology to do this. She is a gentle horse, has the technology and says "harness me and you have harnessed technology that you couldn't otherwise have." Harness this one, my friend, and ride the wave of the future to increased income and profit. Jump on the bandwagon; it's coming down your street. It is powered by Amazon and there's still a lot of room for people who have a vision and a passion to see their vision materialize.

If you are not an author and don't want to be one, you can also sign up with Amazon to sell just about any product you may have, or have access to. Their arrangement for sellers of products is also extremely generous and quite easy to start.

To sell products, you will have to ship them to customers yourself. These products can be something that you make, or that you buy at wholesale. If a product is more your style, check out this opportunity. Just go to www.amazon.com and at the bottom of the page, click on become a seller.

Did I say that Amazon's site gets about FIVE MILLION unique visitors per day? Yep, it's true. That's five million buyers that have an opportunity to see your book or product EVERY DAY! I dare you to try to get that kind of exposure anywhere else, unless you are wealthy enough to do what Amazon does on your own and have many years to wait and lots of money to spend, to get the word around the world. These 5 million people per day are Amazon customers that they will share with you. This opportunity is tremendous!

Full disclosure: My only connection with Amazon is as an author and customer. They do not pay me to promote their programs. I am simply sharing what I've learned, for our mutual benefit. I earned my money when I wrote this book and collected it when you bought it. That's it. Thank you very much for your support.

After you finish this book, please leave a review. It will help other people decide if this book will be worthwhile for them.

Partnering with Amazon is a great way you can harness the technology of today and the future to significantly boost your income, whether you sell books with valuable information, or products that deliver excellent value to your and their customers.

Ideas to Help You Write Your Book

Every action we take in life begins with a thought. We must think before we act, and the more carefully we think about an action, the more effective and successful the action usually turns out to be. Let's think about a plan for your book.

1. Determine to whom you are going to write; who your audience is. The more specific you are about this, the easier your future decisions in writing will be, such as the kind of examples that will be understood by your audience. This will influence your selection of words, colloquialisms, etc. You cannot write a book in a reasonable time that will appeal to everyone, and time spent trying to address those who are not interested in your offering is a waste of time and mental energy.   Identify   a   specific   audience.

2. With your specific audience in mind, specify your subject matter and determine the scope, the depth of information you intend to deliver. Will it be an overview book, or will you go into deep detail? You need to set limits in order to produce the book in a reasonable amount of time.

3. Create your title. Creating your title first, gives you a guide to follow. A good title should tell potential readers what the book will give them. Example: ***Everything You Want to Know About Money*** suggests a very different product than ***Everything You Need to Know About Budgeting Your Money.*** Take your time and craft your title carefully. The title is what will get buyers of books interested in considering what you have to say. Once you dedicate yourself to carefully crafting your title, ideas will come, some ideas will seem like the answer, but keep thinking and

imagine your book's content and new ideas will come. It may even take days to settle on the title. If you write without a title, you have no real guide to guide you and the resulting product may well be disjointed and confusing, even though it may be packed with good (disorganized?) information. As you work on your title, be very, very sure to include your major keyword. I'll have more on keywords shortly.

4. Select and write down the topics you intend to cover in your book. The items in this list of topics will become chapters. From the list of topics, you will then craft chapter titles (headlines) that grab the reader's attention and help him or her *want* to continue reading. Use the opportunity to offer something valuable, or to create curiosity about the chapter.

5. Under each topic, list, in a word or two, the details that you intend to cover and/or explain. This is where you will have to discipline yourself to stay within the limits of your intended scope of the book. You will need to give all the necessary details, but avoid the temptation to try to tell everything you know about the subject, or your book will probably never get finished. Be complete, be thorough, but avoid perfectionism. It will never be perfect, therefore striving for perfection will probably ensure that your book never gets completed. This list of details will become subsections within the chapters, or paragraphs. You may like to use your detail list as subheadings, again carefully crafted to retain the reader's interest.

One important thought on choosing your topic that I'd like to offer for your benefit is that it doesn't have to be original. It just has to be your own. If you wait until you think of a topic that no one has written about before, you'll probably wait forever. That won't make you any money. What you need is any topic that interests you that you know something about, or have an angle on, or thoughts to present that few, if any authors have written about.

The nature of books and magazine articles is to present what you know about an old subject that not everyone knows. Even if everyone knows about it, you may have an insight that is widely under emphasized, that you can expound on in a new way. For example, I have six books on the topic of time management on my desk, not counting what's on my bookshelf. They're all on the same topic, yet each one is different. Each one enhances the challenges to my mind on the subject. Each one of those books, all on the same subject, has the potential to teach me a principle that I may be able to apply to a different subject. Each one has influenced me in some different way and broadened the scope of my general understanding which I could combine with experiential knowledge gained elsewhere that will help me create a refreshing new book, for a particular niche or audience. Reading books is kind of like stamp collecting. You don't stop collecting stamps from a given country because you already have one; no you keep collecting to enhance your collection and make it more valuable.

The Importance of Keywords

If you publish your book on Amazon, via Kindle Direct Publishing and/or Create Space for printed books, your book must be appealing to the robots that will scan and classify the content of your book. Even if you publish with a traditional publisher, in the final analysis, your book will be available for sale on the internet, therefore, internet protocols still apply.

The internet is organized by keyword. That means that you must be keyword conscientious as you write. The effective use of your keywords will influence the words that you put onto the paper, uh, I mean screen. Here's how I suggest you handle the keyword situation:

1. Select a major keyword and two or three minor ones. Choose your keyword(s) by popularity, by the number of searches done on the keyword you are interested in. There are free keyword selection tools available, just search and select one to research your keyword for popularity. The point is that your keyword is eligible for selection to be presented to the searcher when anyone searches for your keyword. For example, if a person searches using the word "Author" in any context, this book is eligible for presentation.

2. Work your keyword(s) into your title. This is a must, as it is a criterion that will help rate your book more highly by the robots and will influence the level of promotion it gets from Amazon's automated system. Greater promotion will translate to increased sales.

3. Be sure and use your keyword several times in your introduction.
    CAUTION: Don't overdo it. Be sure your use of keywords is consistent with the context, and don't create a context to enable you to over-use your keyword. That is considered keyword spamming and is rejected by the 'bots. You will also want to use your keyword(s) appropriately throughout the book, but it may not appear in every chapter. It is not necessary for it to be everywhere, but it should always be

used   where   it   is   appropriate.

Example: My keywords for this book are: "money," "author," and "cash." This book talks a lot about money and being an author, both popular keywords. They do enjoy lavish use in the book, but are always properly used, not over-used and used in context.

Expand Your Search Results Even More

You can have a better chance at being found in the search results for your keyword(s) by using the examples and quotes of famous people related to your topic. This is helpful for emphasizing your points for the reader and also make your work a candidate to be reported in the search results for the names of the people or businesses you cite or quote. The same holds true for businesses and corporations whose products you may have occasion to recommend.

Example: In this book, I have used the names of Microsoft and Apple, in context to deliver additional information to the reader. That also helps search results. If someone searches for "Apple stock price" they may get my book in their results. I also used Warren Buffett's name and some of his sage advice for the same two reasons. If Joseph Kowalski had said the same things that Warren Buffett said, I would still quote Mr. Buffett, for obvious reasons.

If your book is going to be *How to Protest Peacefully and Get Results,* you may choose to include some quotes from Martin Luther King, Jr. or from Ghandi, for example. If you're writing on the title *How to Speak Publicly with Confidence*, you may cite the work of, and quotes from, James Malinchak or Zig Ziglar. If your topic is perseverance you might find value for your readers in the works of

Louis Zamperini or the movie about his life, **Unbroken,** or Daniel (Rudy) Ruteiger from the movie **Rudy.** This list of ideas could continue for a long time, but I think you get the point. If I can do it, you can do it.

These suggestions are really rather simple. They represent a one-time investment of a little mental energy that can pay off throughout the life of your book. Just start with a plan, then take action and work the plan, then your book will begin to take shape right before your eyes.

More Ways to Contribute to Your Book's Success

While it is true that you can write your book, format it for Kindle and Create Space on Amazon, and that they will promote your book and offer it for sale to five million visitors per day, this system alone may not garner all the sales you desire.

In the interest of complete disclosure, I would like to inform you that that system is easy and has amazing potential for something that easy. It is also true that easy things are less valuable than the more difficult. It is as if life was a person and is watching your every move and meting out rewards in accordance to the passion and commitment you display.

You can "go the extra mile", if you choose and boost your chances of having a best seller significantly by doing some additional marketing yourself. Best-selling authors do it. You may want to follow their example, but you may be short on time and need to settle for Amazon's services as your exclusive marketing effort. That's O.K.; it's just not the way to *maximize* sales. As previously noted, the level of promotion from Amazon and the resulting sales of your book will depend on the level of your adherence to the electronic medium in use.

Writing a good book that delivers great value to the reader will make you some nice money, but very rarely does that make the author rich. The major benefit is the exposure that it gives you, as your book serves to introduce you to the people who make up your market. It also opens the door to you for paid speaking engagements. Having an authoritative book published does wonders to position you in your niche or market.

Best-selling authors actively participate in the selling of their books through events like book signings and speaking. They also pitch their books to businesses, libraries, colleges and universities that are good prospects to buy multiple copies. Another marketing possibility is to give your book, or a part of it, away to businesses that it serves for use as a simple guide or handbook for executives, employees, or whomever is best positioned to apply and benefit from it. This will keep your name and your book's title in the forefront of your client's, or prospect's, minds, while delivering value to them. That will increase the chances that they will call you when they need your product or service. It will increase the chances for you to receive a great reception when you or your sales people call on them.

Other offline marketing opportunities are sending out press releases, in an effort to get interviewed about your book and its value, by magazines, on radio and television. If you can create interest in your topic among the media and pitch them according to their protocol, you could do an interview in print or on television or radio that would do wonders to increase sales.

Of course, there are also myriad online opportunities you can use, should you decide to do some additional marketing. You can put your book on your website, mention it judiciously, in accordance with the appropriate protocols on social media and blogs, use it as a focal point to create your own blog or even your own audio or video podcast.

Summary

Your level of involvement will affect the significance of your results. No one else will be as passionate about the value of your book as you are. No one else cares as much as you do about how well it sells. Those are just the facts.

There is no question that you can write a book and get it published on Amazon, get free marketing and access to a tremendous audience that will provide a level of success commensurate with the diligence of your planning and the effectiveness of your delivery. It is also unquestionable that a higher value of content and a more intense promotion of that value will reward you with greater value.

As I will say in the leadership book that I have just started working on, no matter what you do in life, the results you get are dependent upon your level of passion and commitment, and the effort you put into any given project.

Some Final, Friendly Points to Consider:

- Select a topic that you are passionate about and committed to and create a compelling title
- Write down your goals for the book and review them before each writing session
- Write down your goals for the writing process, including time limits
- Plan carefully and thoroughly – good products are always built upon strong foundations
- Make your presentation interesting and easy to read

- Be forthright – don't hide your point in a pile of unnecessary or ambiguous words (unless, perhaps ambiguity is your subject)
- Limit your scope – don't try to tell everything you know about your topic
- Reduce words and add value wherever possible and reasonable
- Your goals should be realistic and attainable, as you operate within the constraints of your circumstances in life
- Small sections of your book can become blog posts; conversely, a collection of blog posts can become your book
- Read more than you write; much more – the books you don't read can't help you. Read what interests you, observe and note how the author uses, words, phrases and punctuation. Learn from the good ones.
- Record your thoughts, ideas and plans in a journal as you start planning; review it often
- Most famous authors are famous because they used their books as platforms to launch other related careers, such as public speaking. Mark Twain preferred to write, but when a sideline business bankrupted him, he dedicated himself to speaking in order to pay off all he owed. It worked.
- Be VERY CAREFUL who you tell about your ambitions. There are a lot of people who make it their business to make sure you fail in yours.

May your imagination be vivid, your spelling correct, your diligence sufficient that you may take your place on the bookshelves of discerning readers next to celebrated authors such as Hemmingway and Twain.

Chapter 4

Opportunities of the Future

To borrow from the Firestone Tire Company, this is "Where the rubber meets the road."

What are the opportunities of the future? No one knows! The best we can do is try to focus on blurry images we see on the horizon, do a little digging in the news to see if anyone is showing their hand. I will share what I've seen and what my digging has turned up.

One image that is coming into focus for me is 3D Printing. This technology is expanding rather quickly. Just a short time ago, it made the evening news and was mentioned briefly in a couple of places I found on the internet. My recent findings reveal that it is now being used to make parts for custom airplane interiors, from plastic, I think. 3D printing technology is also expected have a very bright future in the manufacture of prosthetics.

That scoop tells me that there is a potential for 3D Printing to become a manufacturing medium. That is HUGE! That tells me that in a few years the technology could displace present day manufacturers of almost anything, especially plastics. History tells me that as it becomes more widespread, expenses will drop, as production increases, and the method becomes more popular.

Just stop for a minute and think, if it does expand as I just described, about the possibilities if you were to own stock in a 3D Printing company; how about a 3D printer manufacturer; better yet, what if you had stock in a company that makes the parts for all the companies that manufacture 3D printers? The enormity of its future possibilities appear to be absolutely spectacular!

To help you put this idea into perspective, where would you be today if you had purchased stock in Microsoft or Apple 10 years ago?

Ten years ago, you would have paid just under $500 for 20 shares of Microsoft. At today's market closing those 20 shares would have sold for $957.58 Microsoft did not outperform the market very much at all. That's not a bad return, but not that good either.

For Apple on the same day, 10 years ago, you could have bought 94 shares for $500. Today's price would have brought $12,335.22. That's a great return, 24 TIMES the original investment in just 10 years!

What made the difference? I can't say exactly, but I would think that the difference was in management, company policies and marketing, with emphasis on marketing. With a choice like that, why would anyone have picked Microsoft? That difference is very subjective, depending upon the buyer's preferences, risk tolerance, view of the future and many other personal considerations.

With your money in either of these stocks, you would have been better off than holding the cash. Without question, the American dollar has been losing value over those same ten years. With that money in a savings account, with interest rates below 1% you would still be losing buying power, and that is what money is for; to buy the things you need and want. We all want as much buying power from our money as possible, and for good reason.

While the dollar did not weather the recession of '08 very well, both of these stocks have done well. The key to being able to pick Apple over Microsoft lies in research. Thorough research includes evaluating the management, company policies, marketing savvy of management, their plans, its leadership effectiveness, opportunities for the future and how much money they have for implementing future plans, among others.

If you have never bought and sold stocks before, you should study the subject thoroughly before committing any money to the market. To get you started in your study, just go to a brokerage firm's website, read the news (news drives the market), and read recommendations. Get into the culture and you will soon learn what to look for. It is important, but it is not difficult.

John S. Rhodes has a short book on finances on Amazon called *Money Leaves Clues*- 27 Secrets to Financial Freedom. The book is short, direct and to the point. Mr. Rhodes gives some insights into investing in the stock market very safely. Check it out; you may like it.

Investing in the stock market is how you can take the income you earn and make it work for you. Carefully invested in safe companies for the long term, it will multiply in buying power. You need to pick companies that have great leadership and management. You need to buy quality, and if possible, at a bargain price. You need to go for the long term. It's safer and much simpler. You also need to go for quality, rather than price. Occasionally, you can find quality companies at a bargain price and that's always nice, but focus on quality and plan to hold for the long term.

As Warren Buffett said, "You can't have a baby in a month by getting nine women pregnant." Some things just take time.

Let's take a closer look at the stock market.

Chapter 5

Is the Stock Market Safe?

In the United States, the stock market was established in 1792. It has been doing business for a long, long time.

Here is what Warren Buffett, America's most famous investor and second richest man, with a net worth of $70 Billion said about the market.

> *In the 20th century, the United States endured two world wars and other traumatic and expensive military conflicts; the Depression; a dozen or so recessions and financial panics; oil shocks; a flu epidemic; and the resignation of a disgraced president. Yet the Dow rose from 66 to 11,497.*

Not only has the market survived all those challenges, plus the recession of 2008, but it has prospered, as Mr. Buffett showed in the quote above.

With that said, there are safe ways to invest in the market, and there are other ways, with varying increased levels of risk as well. Each investor should assess his or her tolerance for risk, study the market and carefully research the stocks that they find interesting, track the stock(s) of interest for a while and then invest in stocks that they are comfortable with. In the end, you are responsible for your investment decisions. There are no guarantees. If that bothers you, either you need to learn more, or just stay out of the stock market.

Two safe methods of investing in stocks are No load index mutual funds and buying individual stocks that you hold for the long term, and the longer the better, generally speaking.

Warren Buffett's words of wisdom on the subject of risk are

Risk comes from not knowing what you are doing.

A long time ago, an old, trusted friend said to me

You can learn to do anything you want by reading books.

My friend Dan was right. I have learned many, many things over the last 45 years that I wanted or needed to learn by reading books. The hard part for me was considering that assembly instructions are books.

If you don't know what to do, you can always study to learn what to do. When you think you have a viable plan, search the stock listings, do your research, select a stock, then put that stock, or those stocks on a watch list and follow them for a while. If their performance is satisfactory to you, check the news on the company for anything negative that might drive the price down, then, buy according to your conscience. If there is news that you think will drive the share price of a top quality company down, and if the reason is not damning, you will do better if you wait for the price to drop, then buy and hold for the long term. With good companies, a price drop is almost always followed by an increase, and increases are almost always followed by a drop. The larger the increase or decrease is, the sooner it will be followed by a "correction." That is unless there was a solid reason for the large price change.

If you take on too much risk for your personality, as I once did, and lose, you will likely lose your appetite for investing in stocks and miss the opportunity, if you don't develop a new, safer plan.

The purpose of investing in the stock market, for our purposes, is to take some of your income, especially newfound income and allow it to grow your original investment so that later when you use the money, you will have more buying power than you would have without the investment. The dollars you receive when you sell some of your stock in, say, twenty years will be dollars of reduced value, but if you've made good choices in good companies, you will have more dollars than you would if you had just saved them at pitiful interest rates.

You can then use those additional dollars to buy the things you need and want. With this plan, as the value of dollars drop, the number of dollars you control increases, offsetting the loss of value of each dollar.

While loss is possible, depending upon your choice of stocks, your increase in value, through increased quantity will probably keep up with the loss of value, or it can significantly exceed the rate of loss, as in the Microsoft and Apple examples. This allows you to protect your buying power; that is what counts.

There is a very important principle about the stock market that every investor should be aware of, but many are not. That principle is that **_you will never take a true loss until you sell; likewise you will never receive a true gain until you sell._**

After you invest in a fund or stock, with money you are willing to forget about for many years, it will fluctuate. Overall, you want stocks with a trend that moves higher and higher, in spite of the downturns. That is just how business works. If you continue to hold the stock after a downturn, it will rise again, and you will "make money." If you panic and sell in a downturn, you will lose real dollars. That's why you need to hold it for the long term. Until you are near the time that you planned in advance to start selling, don't worry about it. If anything, when the stock goes down, if the company is still solid, that's a good time to buy more stock, not to sell. Taking a look at the chart of Wal-Mart's (WMT) is a good example of how a stock fluctuates as it continuously climbs over the long term.

Here's some more of Warren Buffett's wisdom:

> It's far better to buy a wonderful company at a fair price than a fair company at a wonderful price.

> Only buy something that you'd be perfectly happy to hold if the market shut down for 10 years.

As we noted earlier, a purchase of Apple or Microsoft stock ten years ago would have grown your money much better than a bank savings account, or Certificates of Deposit. One would have been a very good buy, the other would have been a stellar investment, with Microsoft doubling your money and Apple multiplying it 24 times. Some hint of the difference could probably have been identified in the beginning through careful research of the companies.

What happens when you buy stock is that you become a part owner in the company you select. The money you pay for the stock goes to the company to fund its operations and future development. Good companies are always striving to impress stockholders. Of course, some succeed, others do not. Research carefully. Warren Buffett always suggests focusing on the quality of the company and buying good companies. He has said that if it is a good company, it doesn't matter when you buy it, for long term investment. If, when the time is right for you, the price on that good company's stock has dropped, so much the better; you get a good company at a bargain price. A reduced price on top quality goods is always a good thing. If you have to pay top dollar for a good company, it will still grow your money over the long term. Quality is the important thing.

There are three families on the Forbe's Richest Families list, meaning that they are worth over one billion dollars. They got there by buying stock in Warren Buffet's Berkshire Hathaway company, or by selling businesses to Mr. Buffett in return for Berkshire stock. They got the stock and held it over the long haul, while Warren Buffett, America's most famous investor and second richest man, worked for them. That is what stock in a good company can do.

I have recently researched Berkshire Class B stock. I noted its slow, steady growth, with an occasional drop. Over the last 20 years, it would have been a conservative money making investment.

For my purposes, I did determine, however, that Mr. Buffett's stock is not appropriate for me, for the future because Mr. Buffett is "Old school." Let me explain why I backed away.

Mr. Buffett has stated clearly on more than one occasion that he will not invest a company or business sector that he doesn't understand. He has also made it known that he doesn't understand technology. My objective analysis of the way I think the winds are blowing indicates that growth in the long range future is going to be technology based *and* detrimental to traditional "Old school" businesses, as I stated previously. That's just my opinion, but my research tells me that I am not alone.

Obviously, advice from an old sage not to invest in something you don't understand is very sound advice. That policy has served Mr. Buffet very well over the years, but now it appears that the tremendous effects of the technological revolution are in the process of overtaking Mr. Buffett's sound policy. That is what we call change; and change is inevitable. Nothing lasts forever. Consider that newspapers used to be the primary news vehicle.

Today they are all but obsolete. Empires are built, they stand for a while, then they decline.

If, and this is a big if, technology does reduce the profitability of the old businesses of the era of the industrial revolution, the return from the companies Berkshire invests in will, in my opinion, inevitably moderate or decline. That is not what I want from my investments over the next 20 years. For that reason, and with all due respect and admiration for Mr. Buffett's expertise, I think I will profit more if I travel the new road, while applying the wonderful old school values that Mr. Buffett has taught me, to my investment in companies that I think will control the future. That tells me that I must learn about technology and the companies involved with it, so that I understand it.

There is much room for me to grow in my understanding of tech companies, so I must do a lot of learning before I put any money down on those stocks. I will say, though, that I am very interested in 3D printing. I don't know what I will do yet, but I am interested and researching that field.

There is one source of market information for research that I really like. It is the Motley Fool's stock advisor. Those folks seem to be really long on talent and investment savvy. They also have a sort of contrarian outlook. They know that what most people are doing is wrong, and they have a consistent track record of picking winners that significantly outperform the market. Outperforming the market is basically necessary to cause your money to grow best, as the market's average performance tends to just keeps pace with inflation, or slightly better. Even returns at the market average will

> "The woman who follows the crowd will usually go no further than the crowd. The woman who walks alone is likely to find herself in places no one has ever been before." – Albert Einstein

usually keep your money from losing buying power, but that's about all.

If you are contemplating entering or exploring the market, I would suggest that you explore their website at www.fool.com I have no business relationship with The Motley Fool, other than that I subscribe to their Stock Advisor newsletter. I am just one of their happy customers.

All you need in order to invest in the stock market is about $500 to open an account, the willingness to research thoroughly the companies that interest you, make an informed decision and select good, strong companies that have a good outlook for the future, and then invest. You don't have to be rich to start. If you do it right, you could go in with little and come out very rich. The stock market is the only place I know of that the everyday person can invest to reap rewards of increased buying power. I am so fully convinced of that, that I am almost constantly debating with myself about whether I am better off investing in the stock market, or continuing to invest in my business as an author and leadership speaker. The answer I keep arriving at is that investment in my business will produce a great short term profit, then part of that needs to be invested in stocks for additional profit over the long haul.

Remember, it is not very likely that you will take a real loss in the market, if you have picked a good company unless you choose to sell when the price of the shares you own is down.

In his book *Money Leaves Clues*, John S. Rhodes reveals that he thinks, as I have suggested here, that buying individual stocks is quite risky. It is obvious that he and I have different outlooks on this point. I suggest that if my idea sounds too risky to you that you spring for three bucks and buy his book, as you begin to explore the possibilities. Consider all the angles, and do your own thinking. With all stock market investing, you are responsible for your choices, just as you are if you choose not to invest there.

If you feel that the stock market is too risky for you or if you will be uncomfortable while your money is invested there, your safe solution is to not enter that market. Intolerance of the risk at any level of commitment will probably have strong adverse effects on your outlook for the future, your sense of financial security and even your family life. I strongly suggest that you carefully consider your tolerance for risk and set a written goal not to exceed the level of commitment you are comfortable with, even if that number is zero.

If you choose not to invest in the stock market, it will be more difficult for you to increase the quantity of your money in order to offset its continuing loss of value. You can still theoretically do that by earning more money, which will require you to expend more mental and/or physical energy to produce the increased amount of money you will need in the future for your old age. As discussed earlier, you can increase your income by writing books and publishing on Amazon, or by selling products on Amazon. If the stock market is not for you, then adding those ideas to your present activities might be a good answer for you. Just keep on writing or selling products. Being comfortable with the status of your money is also valuable, so do what you are comfortable with.

By way of review, up to this point, I have shown you how the technological revolution makes it possible for you, for anyone, to harness technology at a low level and create additional income, using the highest levels of technology, with little or no monetary expense. I have expounded at some length to remind you of a way to grow that income to increase your net worth, increase the buying power of the money you have and set yourself up for a more prosperous and secure future. In case you are not sure that the stock market is for you, let's take a look at another way to make an honest buck that can increase your productivity while eliminating the uncertainties of the stock market.

Chapter 6

Another Money Maker

The third and final way to let technology increase your income that I will discuss with you has been around for a long time, but still is part of the "New School." Actually, it is a sort of hybrid; a cross between the old and the new ways. It requires more work on your part, is more complex than the plans discussed in previous chapters, but can still boost your income. Just because this idea is not very appealing to me, doesn't mean that it won't be appealing to you.

What I am referring to is contracting or telecommuting.

As a contractor, you could sell your skills to any company that you can connect to via the internet. If you are an accountant, you could do book work for a company, using your own equipment and charge more than if you were hired as an in-house employee. Contractor status, however, would eliminate employee status that allows you to receive employee benefits from the employer. As a contractor, you are an independent business owner and would be responsible for handling your own taxes and benefits, such as health insurance.

In order to start a business as a contractor, you will, in most cases, have to purchase the hardware that you will need to deliver your service to a business. Of course, you may already have the necessary equipment. Once you have the equipment you will have to drum up the business by contacting businesses, or individuals who could benefit from the service you provide. The service(s) you could provide range across the entire spectrum of what is possible on the internet.

You could provide graphic design services, a writing service, a service creating presentations for speakers or salespeople, even using photos and media provided by the client. I know a 14 year old boy who creates electronic memory albums for funerals from photos provided by the families of their dearly departed. He builds the albums digitally and adds music of the customer's choosing to create impressive presentations at the funeral or memorial service.

The possibilities are endless; electronic year books, prom memories, high school sports highlights, book keeping, business letter writing could be combined with a mailing service, billing, setting appointments for busy salespeople. The possibilities are limited only by our imaginations. With these and any other services, you must be able to provide a strong value for the client. If your brand doesn't deliver strong value, you will kill the brand. Profits are derived by adding value to the market. As a mentor of mine, Jim Rohn says, "Wages will earn you a living; profits will earn you a fortune."

The other hybrid method of increasing your income utilizing technology is telecommuting. This is simply a situation in which you make an arrangement, as an employee, with your boss in a traditional business to do your work at home; communicating and submitting your work via the internet. Frequently, such situations require the telecommuting employee to be in the office part time, or to attend meetings. Some agreements allow the employee to work from home 100% of the time.

This method is simple, after you've convinced your boss. You are still an employee, with the financial arrangement that you have negotiated with your employer, but you work from home. In my opinion, the best agreements for remote working are usually those that pay for your production, rather than your time. In such a situation, a person who formerly spent eight hours per day in the office can optimize his time working from home by eliminating physical commuting time as well as unexpected visits from co-workers and other unscheduled interruptions. That can make it possible to produce a day's work in only a few hours. The time saved could prove valuable in setting you up to be able to create a new stream of income by following one of the ideas I have previously mentioned, or another idea that your imagination produces.

Telecommuting could be a valuable tool to set you up to eliminate commuting time, consolidate work time, maintain your present salary and have time during daylight hours to pursue an independent business of your own, creating an opportunity for you transfer yourself from wage earner to profit earner. It could allow you to "Moonlight" during the day, without losing your paycheck.

Chapter 7

The Biggest Obstacle

This one will probably make you think that I am a mind reader, or that I have been spying on you. I am not a mind reader, and I haven't been spying on you; it is just that I am old, I have been around a long time, I have been observant and have learned a lot.

Our biggest obstacle is also our best asset; our brains. Consider this quote, that I don't know whom to credit for:

> Do you remember who you were before the world told you who you should be?

Not very many can answer "yes" to that question. As a result, far too many unique, talented people run around with a mind full of trashy thinking that they have allowed others to plant there. I am talking about trash like "I can't," "I wish I were like someone else," "That's for the experts," or any other junk that you feed yourself that holds you back. Some people want to fail, but I don't think they'll be reading this book. Since you are reading this book, I believe that you can do anything your imagination suggests; do you? If you don't believe you can do a thing, you can't.

Consider the story of Roger Bannister. From the beginning of human history until the middle of the 20th century, it was a well known, proven and accepted fact that no human could run a mile in less than four minutes. In 1954, Roger Bannister did it! After Bannister accomplished the feat, others followed and broke his record. The difference is in the belief. One man imagined something contrary to public opinion and expertise, believed his imagination, took the necessary steps to accomplish, stepped out in front of the nay-saying world, and persevered until he accomplished his goal.

You can turn the imaginations of your mind into reality, but you must believe you can before you will.

Our Declaration of Independence truthfully says that "All men are created equal." I know that's true because we all came into this world naked, squalling, toothless and empty-headed.

Why is it then that some people succeed and others fail? It is because not all of these folks who are equal at the starting gate pursue opportunity equally. Some run the race to win; others just hang out on the track. If you are just hanging out on the track and are still above ground, it is not too late to get in the race; just take a deep breath, stretch your muscles and brain for a little warm up, set your eye on the finish line and get going at your best pace for an endurance run. You CAN do it, if you will. Listen to Nike:

Just do it!

Your brain is your most powerful tool; it can also be your weakest link, if you don't feed it good information. That is a choice we each have to make for ourselves.

While some of you are on top of the world, chomping at the bit to move forward, others of you are going through trials and tribulations; think financial reversal, divorce, over work, information overload and many other negative things.

Your future is in front of you, not behind you. Look ahead. Most of the successful people whom we know of, we know because they became successful; because they endured those same sorts of negative things in their lives, but they looked ahead, kept their eye on their goals, the finish line, and kept on running. They ignored naysayers and didn't quit. Everyone knows that Babe Ruth hit over

700 home runs, but few know that he also struck out over 1,300 times.

Get this. According to Kim Komando, Elvis Presley was advised to go back to truck driving after a less than spectacular performance at the Grand Ole Opry. You can read Kim's story for yourself at this link:

http://www.komando.com/small-business/302981/one-thing-that-makes-a-difference-between-success-and-failure

Kim's entire article is right on the money.

She is known as America's Digital Goddess and sure helps people understand technology. As you can see from that article, she also ventures into other areas. The article contains a list of well-known authors, entertainers and sports figures who overcame rejection before we knew them.

What I like about Kim is that she obviously thinks for herself and strives to help her audience with valuable information. I recommend her as an example and guide to follow, as you begin your journey to harness technology as you set out to help others and make a profit for yourself.

These opportunities are not just for others; they are for YOU also. There is room on this bandwagon for anyone. It is just that the longer we wait, fewer good seats are available.

This is as good a place as any for me to thank Kim Komando for her help with this book. I listened to her radio program on Saturday, April 11, 2015. A man called in with questions about publishing e-books. She answered his question and promised to put more information on her website on that topic.

The things she said taught me that my mental approach (I was thinking too much "Old School") was not the best. At that time I had a book about managing activity using the 80/20 Principle in the works. Kim's advice taught me to put that on hold and write a smaller book about something else that I know about, that lots of other people don't know about. The result was that I put 80/20 on the back burner and started writing one on the pitfalls of retirement planning. That book is in the works, but for the moment, it is also on the other back burner while I write this one. Thanks, Kim. I really appreciate your work, and your help.

Please let me continue on this related rabbit trail. It's almost off topic, but not really, because it is all a real life example of how someone (me) is actually doing what I have suggested above.

After I spent about 3 hours per day writing on the Retirement Planning book, I attended a webinar (see the technology?) presented by Steve Harrison, with two authors who have over 140 books selling on Amazon. The topic was about how to publish a book on Amazon and make money at it. I was all ears as I listened to John S. Rhodes and Jay Boyer explain how they did it. It was a great webinar. I already knew how to do everything that I've taught in this book, but I listened anyway, and they fleshed out some details for me. Never stop learning; never stop reading.

The purpose of the webinar was for them to give away some valuable information that would help authors do better, as well as to give them a chance to sell their product which consists of technological tools to help authors produce a better book, get more highly rated and sell more. I bought the goods, put the retirement planning book on the other back burner, slept on all that information for one night, then the next morning the title of this book came to mind and I made a rough outline, called on my experience and the experiences of others, and began writing. My goal is to have this book selling on Amazon by June 30.

That is a smart investment on my part. Here's my strategy: Get a book that is short and loaded with valuable information selling on Amazon, so that my name starts to be recognized, and sales begin to be made. That will also bring me some income as I continue writing my other two books that are lengthier and will take longer to write. This strategy will help shorten the time I have to wait to receive a return on my investment of time and knowledge.

Do you see? I eat my own cooking. What you are reading is the result of me doing exactly what I am suggesting you do. Unlike Agatha Christie, Zane Grey and the many other authors Kim mentioned in her article, Amazon doesn't reject manuscripts of decent, legitimate books! No, they solicit them, they print them, publish them, market them, handle sales and collections and pay better than any of those old school, known for rejections publishers ever did! Technology is opening new, exciting opportunities, folks. Get on the bandwagon if you want to expand your horizons and your wallet.

I also need to take just a moment, right here, in front of you to thank Jay Boyer and John S. Rhodes for their help in driving home the enormity of the opportunity that I am writing about here.

Again, I would like to thank you for buying this book, and I sincerely hope that some of the information you've found here will help and encourage you to find more of whatever you are looking for.

If you are a student feeling crushed by student loans, you probably already embrace the technology, but may need a guide to show you a viable way to cash in on it. In the beginning I explained how. If you need to, go back and review that, then just do it.

Perhaps you think because you are young, you don't have enough knowledge to write a book full of valuable information. Consider your experiences, my friend. You could write about your childhood, your neighborhood; you could do a children's book about your adventures as a child; you could help future college students with a book about campus life, or campus life at a specific university or college.

The books don't have to be really long; they don't have to be a masterpiece that is destined to become a classic. They just have to impart valuable information, or entertain, as in the case of novels.

Even if you can't cook, you could write a cookbook! Think of it. You just need to collect all of the recipes from your mother, grandmothers and friends, give them names, maybe add some photos in the computer, add a little narrative about your enjoyment of some of your favorite recipes and send it to Amazon.

Perhaps you are more like me; old and retired. Maybe you have discovered some of the pitfalls of retirement, noting that your pay never goes up, but prices go up almost daily, or perhaps you are still in college, with student debt piled high, or you may be a wounded veteran (I salute you), or unemployed due to a lay-off or downsizing, you may have a physical impairment or disability that keeps you from holding a "regular job." Whatever your situation, reason or need, anyone can create a new source of income by seizing the opportunity that the technological revolution is presenting to everyone. Every one of you has learned something in life that the rest of us have not, or that we want to read more about. It may be funny, serious, useful or satisfying to the curiosity. It will appeal to many, and they will pay you for that information, but only if you publish it.

Chapter 8

Some Thoughts About Money

Money's only value is that it buys us the things we want and need. Let's explore a little deeper.

Speaking of the American Federal Reserve Note, it has no intrinsic value, meaning that if we could not purchase goods and services with it, it would have no value at all. Ponder that for a moment.

Now, think about this: our money is not backed by anything of value. We Americans no longer have the government's guarantee that we can trade our money for gold or silver, or anything else at a Federal Bank. It is backed only by the good faith of the U.S. Government; a government which is comprised of people; people who have, for the most part, shown themselves to be corrupt, regardless of party affiliation. Can we say with confidence that our money has value because these people, who are caught lying almost daily, who *are* the government say it does?

At this time I think it is safe to say that the reason our money has value is because everyone believes it has value. If a seller is satisfied that $10 is a good trade for his widget and the buyer wants the widget, money has value. If the seller does not agree that the money has value, the buyer cannot buy it with money.

Right now we can see that the confidence of sellers in the dollar is waning. This is demonstrated through ever increasing prices. It is the old supply and demand effect. The more there is of a given item, the less value it has. Put another way, the more common an object, the lower its value.

Through rising prices, sellers are telling the buyers that $10 is no longer sufficient to buy his widget; it now takes $11. That is because the dollar is less valuable than before, when the price was $10. If the value of the dollar remained constant, as well as production methods and practices, the price of the widget would also remain constant, in the absence of greed.

For now, our money is the most accepted medium of exchange; everyone accepts it as having value, but that value is waning because money is losing value; prices are rising. This makes it a tool that we can use wiely, to trade for things that do have intrinsic value.

An item has intrinsic value when it supplies your needs for things that sustain life, such as food, water, shelter, clothing, heat, things such as tools that enable you to work, and things that you want that have value to you.

In the final analysis, money held in your pocket or bank account is losing value. It will buy less tomorrow than today. Considering that, we need to protect our money from loss of value. The only way we, the common people, can do that is to increase the amount of money we have. The best way I have found to do that is to invest it in something that causes the number of dollars invested to increase faster than the value of each dollar decreases. Under present conditions, that is not as difficult as it may sound.

One way to increase the number of dollars you control is to use the information I offered in the early part of this book to increase your income, which is exactly what I am doing with this book, and will do with two other books I have in the works right now, with my speaking business, and with about six more books that I already have ideas for.

As previously discussed, you can imitate what I am doing ; write your own book to increase your income. If that is not your style, you could use modern technology to provide a valuable service to others, such as cover design for authors, any of the ideas I put forth earlier, or best yet, something from your own imagination; something that you can clearly identify a market for. Opening a traditional business however is tough. Most new businesses fail because of a lack of operating capital and marketing ignorance on the part of the entrepreneur. That is why I favor book writing. Amazon will cover my weaknesses in return for only a small share of the sales.

America's wealthy people are, for the most part, people who run their own businesses, not wage earners.

Keeping the serious weaknesses of money in mind, I have found a plan that I like to not only increase income, but also increase net worth, over the long term.

First increase income, or at least allocate some of your present money to the future. This should be money that you are willing to live without for a long time, say five years or more.

Second, invest for the very long term in something stable that, after careful investigation you think will increase the quantity of your dollars faster than your dollars lose value; hopefully much faster. As your income increases, you will want to increase your investments with part of that income. The stock market indexes generally provide a guide, as they tend to outpace inflation slightly. Of course, outpacing inflation by many multiples is possible and much better.

Third, spend the dollars that have increased your net worth through investments to get the things you always dreamed of having. This may be to boost your standard of living in retirement or you may withdraw some of your investment profits along the way to bring vital plans or dreams to fruition. Set written goals and make a definite plan for the multiplication of your money, then follow it.

Dreams transformed into planned, written goals will help strengthen you to willingly delay gratification by spending money. As soon as your money begins to multiply, your discipline will become stronger and your strength will continue to grow. If you insist on instant gratification through the things that money buys, you will soon be consumed by debt, you will not accumulate money for financial security and will face a dismal future in retirement. You need to develop strong, disciplined financial habits in order to achieve financial security. Your finances won't get better until you get better.

By following that plan, your income will increase, you will retain the buying power of your dollars, your net worth will increase and you will be able to participate vibrantly in the economy even in your old age.

Conversely, if you earn money, spend it all, earn more and spend more, as your ability to produce income wanes, your buying power will decrease and you will most likely find yourself struggling to keep afloat financially in old age. That is not to say that you don't spend for the present. You do; just make an intelligent plan and then transfer some present day spending to grow your money for the future. Some things must be bought today, but some things can wait.

Money is tied directly to time and energy. You earn money directly in proportion to the amount of value you add to the market. Return on your invested money is directly related to amount of time you leave it in the investment, and the return also relates to the energy you expend in selecting your investment(s), not to mention the accuracy of your decisions.

When you borrow money, the cost of borrowing (interest) is related to the amount of money involved and the length of time you wish to use that money.

No matter how you cut it, it takes time and energy to acquire money honestly. The amount of time and energy required to earn a dollar is also related to the value of the time and energy, from the viewpoint of the person paying you.

For most of us it is a fact that money comes and goes in small amounts over time. Counting on an expected inheritance or winning the lottery are very long shots and often don't produce the desired results.

Chapter 9

Some Thoughts About Opportunity

Opportunity is also related to time. The dictionary says that "an opportunity is a convenience or fitness of time, place, etc., for the doing of a thing." In other words, an opportunity occurs when various factors come together to make something possible. It occurs when everything necessary is available, and the time is right.

My experiences and 20/20 hindsight have shown me that opportunities also wax and wane. They start small, grow to various sizes, then they wane as they, or the results they produce, become commonplace. Have you ever said to a friend, or to yourself, "Why didn't I think of that, before the market for a good idea became saturated?" Have you ever recognized an opportunity that you wanted to seize, but were unable to fund it?

As I pointed out early on, technology is, at this time, presenting what is probably the most widespread opportunity that I have seen in my long lifetime. At the same time it appears to me that the opportunities of the industrial revolution are waning, not because they weren't good, but because with today's technology they have outlived their usefulness, for the practical purposes of the future. The new, younger opportunity is replacing the old. New and younger generations are replacing the older ones. Technology, combined with the current youthful generations is absolutely changing the way things are done.

Another of my observations of opportunity is that good ones are extremely valuable before they are clearly defined, and that the more clearly they are defined, the less valuable they are.

I'll offer the desktop computer as an example. When most people were saying the computer would never make it and a few visionaries thought it would, the opportunity became very lucrative for those visionaries as well as others who embraced the trend. As they seized the opportunity that was very poorly defined. As their work brought it into focus it was also lucrative for many others who became involved with it, whether their involvement was through investments or actual work. It created new challenges and high paying jobs, as well as creating new opportunities for supporting enterprises.

Now that the computer opportunity is very clearly defined and computers are commonplace, the opportunity to be handsomely rewarded for getting involved by selling computers, for example, has diminished greatly. The market may not be saturated, but it is flooded. Computers have become commonplace and that opportunity is waning significantly because other opportunities have overtaken it and new ones are rapidly following right behind. That is what this book has been about; seizing those new opportunities while the probability of reward is very high.

The technology that has recently become available, that makes it possible for anyone to start a new business for little to no money up front is not yet completely defined. If it were, this book would have no value. The bandwagon that is bringing us this opportunity is moving fast and will pass you by, if you don't make a decision and jump on it before it plays out.

Starting your own full or part time business now, using other people's technology at little to no cost is an opportunity like I never imagined would ever occur. It is your opportunity to enrich the lives of others with your talents, interests, hobbies, knowledge, etc. It is your chance to use your imagination and add value to the marketplace, in return for financial reward.

Chapter 10

Last But Not Least

It is as if I had departed on a scouting mission into unknown territory; that I have been gone many years and have now returned with what I have learned by running out ahead, catching up to people like Warren Buffett and John Rhodes. It is like they allowed me to "stand on their shoulders" and get a look at what is out there farther than I could see from the ground. I have now returned. You may have been in the crowd that saw me depart, or you may have not even been born yet, but now I am back and I bring encouraging news. It is news that can be of immense value to you and me. It is also news that will be

> "There are 309 million people out there that are trying to improve their lot in life. And we've got a system that allows them to do it." – Warren Buffett

meaningless for those who do not do something soon to pursue this opportunity. For those of you who think, make a plan, set goals and take action, this information can help guide you to a fortune.

This book is my attempt to bring the news to you, the everyday man and woman, boy and girl. It is a chance for me to share valuable information that I have learned the hard way that can be helpful to you. It my way of offering you the chance to "stand on my shoulders" and see what's out there, farther than you can see from the ground. I sincerely hope that what you see will motivate you to be successful in improving your lot in life.

"You do things when the opportunities come along. I've had periods in my life when I've had a bundle of ideas come along, and I've had long dry spells. If I get an idea next week, I'll do something. If not, I won't do a damn thing." – Warren Buffett

An Off Topic Bonus for You

Money is not the root of all evil. The people who say that show their ignorance of an important fact, or they reveal their sloppiness in communication.

Having done the digging, tracing the supposed quote back to its origin, I can emphatically state that money is *not* the source of all evil. The quote originates from the Bible, it is found in 1Timothy 6:10 and says:

> *...the love of money is the root of all evil: which while some coveted after, they have erred from the faith, and pierced themselves through with many sorrows.*

The original emphatic statement says the **love** of money. There is a big difference between money and the love of money. Money is, as previously discussed, simply an inanimate tool; a tool that is necessary for our function in daily life. It is the accepted medium of exchange. It is a tricky asset that is constantly losing value.

The love of money, on the other hand, indicates an attitude about money; an attitude that will lead you to support and maybe even participate in evil. The original quote is talking about an attitude that leads to a modus operandi which produces evil behavior.

This serves as a shining example of the widespread misuse of words today, and serves as a prime example of how messages are distorted, or crafted, to end up sending an erroneous message to the reader or listener. Reader, beware. Are you receiving the actual message that you can count on, or someone else's interpretation, or manipulation, of any message?

We have had quite a discussion about the acquisition and use of money because most of us want to be able to buy the things we need and want, and money is the medium that most easily makes that possible. As a medium of exchange, money is also the key to doing good things, such as helping the poor, feeding the hungry, running for office to effect change, starting a business to boost the economy or to stand up to evil by financing a worthy cause or goal.

At the end of the day, though, we need to ask ourselves a question: "Are we just looking for the things that money can buy, or are we looking for happiness?" Are we expecting the things money buys to bring us contentment?

Extra money or the things it can buy will make most people happy, for a moment; or maybe a short season. After that the happiness wears off and we must seek happiness and contentment again. It becomes a never ending cycle, so long as we continue to limit ourselves to physical solutions. "Round and round we go; where we stop, nobody knows." It is a vicious, merciless cycle.

That cycle kept my life in turmoil for my first thirty three years. I searched for happiness in all (the wrong) places that the "experts" said it would be found; money, cars, luxurious living, family. All these things worked, but only for a very short time because money came, then it vanished, cars broke down, luxurious living soon became too cumbersome; it was phony for me. My wife divorced me and took the kids. After that, I hit the bars, but found only excitement for an evening, but no solid happiness.

Not long after separation from my wife, I heard a preacher say that "Jesus Christ paid for all your sins, when he died on the cross; God will never mention your sins because Christ paid the penalty for all of everyone's sins; the penalty of sin is death, and Christ paid it for you, just believe and trust in that and you will be saved. You will be passed from death to eternal life."

That message hit me just right. It was what I needed to hear. I believed and was immediately relieved; it was like the weight of the world was lifted from my shoulders. I was happy at last, but problems still cropped up; I still needed answers, but now I had a new place to look for answers. I could get answers that are solid from the preacher, other members of the church, and from reading the Bible. I found the Bible to be the best because I got different answers to the same questions from different people. Using the King James Bible, I found it to be easy to read and found a simple, multi-faceted, powerful message.

That was thirty five years ago; the Bible still serves me well. It teaches me the truths of life now, just as it did then. It seems to expand as I learn more. Re-reading familiar passages produces new insights & understanding. It is supernatural. Now that I know what God's attitude is, how he looks at me and what he is doing in the world today, not only am I truly happy, I have assurance that I know is real. I have assurance that, for me and other Christians, that going to hell is not an option. I know that Christ supernaturally lives his life through me, and many, many other things that God has done for all of us who believe in Jesus' sacrifice for us.

Briefly, the way it works is that a person trusts Jesus Christ's work on the cross to save him or her. At that moment God "transfers him from the kingdom of darkness into the kingdom of his beloved Son." If that person then reads God's message (the King James Bible), the message "works effectually in us that believe." That "work" transforms the inner man, or woman and gradually changes us for the better. It brings us into alignment with the laws of the universe; it makes us fit properly, like a piece in a puzzle.

A very important key to understanding life is that our lives are lived in the "inner man." The physical body is just a "house" that we live in. It is discarded at death, but we still go either to heaven or hell to continue living; that's the inner person, the spiritual person that cannot be seen with human eyes. Of course, the physical body needs to be cared for, nourished and maintained, but a new dimension opens up to us when we emphasize our inner person in our understanding and decisions.

The bottom line is that God didn't remove bad circumstances from me the moment I trusted Christ; he gave me hope and taught me how to make decisions that lead to better results and gave me the ability to stand strong when life's storms do hit me.

Although I tried to deny it, deep down inside, I always knew that there was life after death and that I would be judged. I didn't like that idea because I knew it would be very unfavorable for me. As a result of my Bible reading, I now know it would have been much worse than I ever imagined, but that God gave me, for just trusting Christ only to save me; the complete opposite of what I deserved, according to his perfect judgement. The Bible calls it "Grace."

If you would like to know more about the wonderful gifts of God that are available to you, just as they are to me, I highly recommend that you go to www.shorewoodbiblechurch.org and listen to messages by Richard Jordan and Alex Kurz. They are the most honest, clearest Bible teachers I have heard in the last 35 years. Their leadership by example is also superb.

Some of you will criticize me for including this in a business book, but the purpose of this book is to help people. This book is based on my experiences and observations and I would be remiss if I failed to share what has been more help to me than anything else. That would be to cheat you; to deliver reduced value. I am compelled to give you the best I have to offer.

Christ lives in me. He is faithful and doesn't leave me when I do business; he holds me up in every area of life. He is more important to me than any of the money or things. You see, Christianity is not a religion; it is a relationship with God, through Christ that is expressed in a lifestyle. Christ has given me deep contentment, whereas money and things only satisfied for a moment. Because he transformed me and my life, because I want to help you, this is the most important part of this book. You may think it is helpful, or you may disagree with me. Either way is fine with me. I am just trying to be helpful and giving it my best shot.

If you haven't already, I hope that you will trust Jesus Christ to make you acceptable to God; that you will find that "peace of God that passes understanding", while the opportunity is available. The opportunity is available to you until the moment you die. The problem is, we don't know when that will be. "Now" is the best time to do most things. Immediate action eliminates procrastination and neglect.

Money is not evil, unless we make it so by loving it, thereby letting it rule, and probably wreck our lives. It is a wonderful servant, but a fearful master.

The opportunity that technology affords today is immense; it is an opportunity that will make a lot of people rich and some who are more savvy and diligent very rich, as they deliver true value to the world and are paid in accordance with the value they add. That money can then be grown, if handled well, and the profits can buy more of the things we need and want. Go for it; you can do it, whoever you are.

Nowhere in this book did I ever say that money and things will deliver lasting happiness and contentment. They won't because they can't. That's God's job.

About the Author

Bob Carpenter is the author of *You Can Make Money as an Author –*  *Jump on the Bandwagon and Cash In Now!* He is also working on two new books, *Retirement Traps – Unanticipated Planning Flaws* and *80/20 in Action – How to Work Less and Accomplish More.*

Bob is also the founder of Bob Carpenter's Leadership & Personal Development, a sole proprietorship formed for the purpose of helping people reach their full personal and leadership potential.

Having honed his leadership skills during a 22 year career in the U.S. Marine Corps and the Army National Guards of Montana and Arkansas, where he served as a professional development trainer for Non-commissioned Officers and as an Intelligence Instructor for senior Non-commissioned Officers and Commissioned Officers, his current goal is to pass his experience and expertise on to the younger generations who are preparing to lead us all into the future.

Bob has been a life-long leader and is a forward thinking alchemist and wordsmith who brings forth original and innovative ideas as well as the tried and proven concepts that have worked in the past that are still ranked among the rules of success today.

In mid-life, Bob became a Christian by the grace of God. The teachings of God's love combined in his heart with his leadership experience to more fully complete his understanding of how to lead people successfully.

Mr. Carpenter possesses a compassionate understanding of the challenges, frustrations and disappointments that we all face, from disease to problems within the family and financial reversal. He cares about the challenges facing younger generations today and having realized that he has answers for many of the young people's problems, he has come out of retirement to lead them forward in difficult and trying times.

Bob has defeated a very deadly cancer, not once, but two times and has now been cancer free for fifteen years.

He now lives "happily ever after" in north central Arkansas with his wife Glocil and their sweet little dog, Jackpot. Bob is available for a limited number of customized workshops, seminars and speaking engagements at schools, businesses, civic groups and churches, as well as for individual personal coaching.

www.ingramcontent.com/pod-product-compliance
Lightning Source LLC
Chambersburg PA
CBHW070949180526
45168CB00003B/1176